Robert
and the Rocket

Leesa Waldron ● illustrated by Lloyd Foye

Copyright © Scholastic Australia Pty Limited, 1997.
All rights reserved. Published by Scholastic Inc.
READING DISCOVERY is a trademark of Scholastic Inc.
First published in 1997 by Scholastic Australia Pty Limited.
Printed in Hong Kong.
ISBN 0-590-76999-5.
Designed by Jobi Murphy.

3 4 5 6 7 8 9 10   05 04 03 02 01 00 99

SCHOLASTIC INC.

New York   Toronto   London   Auckland   Sydney

A lot of noise was coming
from Robert's garage.

Robert was making a rocket.

At last the banging stopped.

Robert was ready to blast off to the moon

in his new red rocket.

Ten 10
Nine 9
Eight 8
Seven 7
Six 6
Five 5
Four 4
Three 3
Two 2
One 1
Zero 0

BLAST OFF!

Higher and higher
went the rocket with Robert inside.

The Earth became smaller and smaller.
Outside it became darker **and darker**.

Robert looked out of his window
and he saw . . .

a falling star.

THUMP! At last he landed.

He was on the moon.

Robert looked out of the window
and to his surprise he saw . . .

A moon monster—a very big moon monster
with one very big eye.
It looked angry.

Robert was so **scared**
that he quickly took off
in his red rocket.

He left the moon and the ugly moon monster
far behind him.

Before you could say 'Monster,'
he was back home again . . .

already planning his next adventure.